Advance Praise for *Achieve Peace of Mind in Your Finances*

A must read for anyone who wants to achieve peace of mind financially. Dr. Sherry Hu is an expert in personal finance, an influential educator, and an inclusive community leader. This book is a result of her passion to give back and help families become financially successful.

—David Haubert, Alameda County Supervisor, Former Mayor of Dublin, California

Dr. Sherry gave our family excellent financial advice for our daughter's college plans. I am so happy to have Sherry help us as this was a new area we have never navigated before. Now I have so much confidence and so does my daughter. Thanks Dr. Sherry!

—Deepak Wilson, tele-comm industry technical director, CA

We met Dr. Sherry while looking for financial guidance to pay for our son's college tuition. She gave us amazing insights and tips into multiple options. I learned a lot from Dr. Hu and strategized accordingly. Dr. Hu went above and beyond in helping us by connecting my son with many amazing opportunities to enhance his leadership skills. Dr. Hu is a true professional and is passionate about helping her clients. A great find!

—Nitin Gupta, Head of AWS Data Platform,
Amazon Web Services (AWS)

I have known Dr. Sherry Hu for several years and have always appreciated her financial acumen. I am so glad that she decided to put her learnings into this book and inspire others to take charge of their finances. The best part is that you don't have to have a financial background to understand this book. A must read for everyone!

—Rashim Mogha, technology leader,
best-selling author and founder of eWOW

I am grateful for Dr. Sherry Hu's guidance on our family's college and financial planning. Due to our busy schedules, both my husband and I do not have the time or knowledge to manage our family finance. Dr. Sherry is a respectful financial planning advisor and has become a friend to our family since we reached out to her for her assistance. She always makes herself available to us when we need her advice. Dr. Sherry has captured her experience and expertise in this book. It is pragmatic, sensible, straightforward and easy to follow. Your family's college and financial planning will benefit from it. Do not miss it!

—Soon Kuek, high-tech executive,
Silicon Valley, CA

I have known Dr. Sherry Hu for several years and she has always been an inspiration to me! No matter what career positions she has taken, she leverages her solid educational background, lifetime of learning, habits of self-improvement, and her hardworking attitude. She has done very well and has become one of the most successful professionals in the area. Achieving Peace of Mind in Your Finances is an incredible book that I would highly recommend to my clients, my family and friends, and anyone else.

—Jack Gelnak, JD, President and CEO,
Premier Wealth Coach

I met Dr. Sherry Hu in an educational event in the San Francisco Bay Area, and I was amazed by the insight and experience she has in college and retirement planning! I was engaged right after. She and her team has helped my family greatly, and we feel complete peace of mind in our student's college funding planning! It is definitely one of the best things that has happened to my family! We are so grateful for her help. You may not have a chance to meet her in person, but you can get a lot of great insider knowledge from her book.

—Dennis Van Wagner, retired executive,
Danville, CA

I am extremely thankful for Dr. Sherry Hu's advice on our family college and financial planning. Dr. Sherry is a brilliant financial planning advisor, and a great friend to our family. I know we can rely on her whenever we need advice and help. This book has important information that will benefit you greatly. Please check it out!

—Swee Kar Seah, parent of a high school
student, Fremont, CA

women taking charge in

MONEY

Achieve Peace of Mind in Your Finances

Dr. Sherry Hu

women lead
PUBLISHING™

Published by Women Lead Publishing

Printed and bound in the United States of America
ISBN: 978-0-9976018-8-6

Dedication

I would dedicate this book to my parents, Mingyong and Xiangfu, who have raised me and taught me important life values: being kind and caring, gratitude, hard work and courage.

And to my family, Tom, Elizabeth and Hubert, whom I have travelled my life with and shared lots of laughter together.

Are you ready to achieve peace of mind in your finances?

Register your book at www.DrSherryHu.com to get a complete collection of online financial resources - workbooks, blogs, financial tips and secrets. Free with purchase of the book, but over $999 of value. Take advantage of this great offer. It will help you achieve peace of mind in your finances.

You will find a clear roadmap that you can take to go from where you are now to financial freedom. You will also have access to educational information and resources that can help you improve your finances significantly.

Table of Contents

Introduction

Finance is a subject everyone inevitably needs to face in their life. There is no way around it. Statistics show that more than 70% of Americans are stressed over their finances. After reading this book and applying its principles to your life, you will have the information and tools to achieve peace of mind in your personal finances.

I have written this book for the middle-class woman, between the ages of 35 and 60. If you are one of these women, you may already have a stable job and have accumulated some assets, such as a 401(k) retirement plan, some savings at a bank, and a brokerage account for stocks. You may also have purchased a house and have children.

Life seems beautiful and peaceful, but from time to time you may still feel anxious about your personal finances.

You wonder, "Why?" You have a good income, but there are just so many bills to pay, among them home mortgage, childcare, vacation, professional clothes, and many types of taxes.

You may have tried to budget, save more, and do regular financial planning, but you still do not feel you have a handle on this.

You may want to improve your personal financial knowledge or seek help from professionals, but even the thought of this can be daunting. There are so many books, so much information, and so many professionals. Where do you start?

And you are already busy with work, family, and social life. Where can you find time?

Deep inside, you know you are lacking peace of mind. You want to change this situation.

Many years ago, I was you. When I was in my mid-30s, I started to feel some apprehension in my life, although I had graduated from a good university with a PhD and had a caring husband, two cute kids, and a decent job.

I was wondering what I missed, sometimes in the middle of the night.

Then I finally figured it out. Like most people at this age, my life had a lot of financial responsibilities. Even a brief thought on what would happen if I lost my job would stress me out. I felt my life was like a mountain full of heavy snow and I was anxious that an avalanche might happen sometime in the future.

I wanted to change this situation. I wanted to figure out how I could successfully plan my personal finances and get peace of mind.

With these goals in mind, I started my exploration and learning process.

During the past decade I have gone through thousands of hours of financial training, and talked to several dozen financial professionals, including traditional financial advisors, institutional investors, CPAs, tax planning professionals, real estate investors, estate planning lawyers, and angel and venture capital investors.

By the end of this decade-long process, I finally figured out the way and I found my passion as a financial planning advisor as well.

This has led me to reach financial freedom and achieve peace of mind in my mid-40s! And I have also helped hundreds of families in their personal finance planning and improved their financial situations.

However, as a personal financial planning advisor, I can only personally help a limited number of people. In order to help more, I decided to write this book.

My hope is that by reading this book you will clarify your needs, learn financial fundamentals, gain access to professionals, read real-life case studies and explore how to get to your own financial peace of mind.

1

Identify your financial needs and goals

As Norman Vincent Peale has said, "All successful people have a goal. No one can get anywhere unless he knows where he wants to go and what he wants to be or do." In this chapter, we will discuss how to identify your personal financial needs and goals in systematic and comprehensive ways. We will look at them in two ways.

The first way is to identify financial needs and goals following six steps: cash flow, debt management, emergency fund, proper protection, asset accumulation and estate preservation.

The second way is to check your personal needs and goals according to different age groups.

Finally, we will explore two common needs for families: college planning and retirement planning.

Six steps to identify your financial needs and goals

Step 1:
What is your current net cash flow?

Net cash flow is calculated by deducting expenses from income. We want to have positive cash flow for our life, which means spending less than what we make. A good rule of thumb is to spend no more than 80%-90% of your income, leaving 10-20% for savings.

For example, a husband brings in $5000 a month after taxes and the wife brings in $3000 a month. If their combined monthly expenses are approximately $6000, the net cash flow formula is $5000+$3000 - $6000 = $2000. That leaves 25% of their income for savings which is a strong saving habit for their family.

If you cannot save at least 10% of your income, you have identified a financial goal to increase your cash flow.

Some ways to increase your net cash flow include reducing your expenses or increasing your income by finding a higher paying job or creating a side hustle to make additional money.

I have always been a good saver starting from a very early age. I inherited this habit from my Chinese parents. From my first paycheck to now I continue to save 20% or more of my income. This good habit has laid a strong foundation for my personal finances and paved the way for me to become financially free and achieve peace of mind.

Step 2:
Do you have debts? Good ones or bad ones?

There are good debts and there are bad debts. Do you know which are good and which are bad? In general, good debts are things like house mortgages and bad debts are things like credit cards with high interest rates.

School loans are good debt as long as the interest rates are reasonable (less than 5%). House mortgages are generally counted as good debt because the house value typically appreciates and the interest rate is reasonable (generally less than 5% and could be as low as 3%).

Car loans are okay as long as the interest rate is good (less than 5%).

The interest rate of credit cards can go up to 20% (and sometimes even higher, a definite red flag). I see some people who take advantage of an offer to get zero or very low interest for a period of time and pay off the debt before the interest climbs to a higher rate, but you need to have savings in another safe account in order to ensure you are capable of doing so when needed.

If you have bad debts, you have identified a financial need to clean them up. One way to do this is to consolidate your credit card debt and follow a plan to pay it off as soon as possible.

Step 3:
How much to save for the emergency fund?

Your goal should be to have three to six months of living expenses in the bank in case of emergencies, such as car or home repairs, losing a job, getting sick and not being able to work, etc. For conservative people, this amount could be six to twelve months. I would say having six months is a good rule of thumb.

In general, your emergency fund should be saved in a bank account or other account with immediate accessibility and no risk of losing value.

If you do not have six months of emergency funds saved, you have identified a need to focus on emergency savings. Find ways to spend less and make more, or move some of your funds from accounts with higher risks, such as stock investments, to an account with no risks, such as banks or a type of permanent life insurance which allows for safe cash value accumulation.

Step 4:
Do you have proper protection?

Protection is very important, especially for young families who have not accumulated a large amount of assets. Different types of insurance (health, auto, property, life, disability, long term care, etc.) can protect families in case of health issues or a big loss.

Also be aware of protection of assets from market risks. There are always market risks. Think about not putting all of your eggs in one basket. Diversification is the golden rule for minimizing risks for asset growth.

As I am writing this book, we are living though one of the largest and most rapid market crashes in the history of the United States due to the coronavirus. At the time of this writing in 2020, the stock market had lost more than 30% and Standard & Poor's 500 Index crashed from 3300 to 2300 in one month's time.

If you have not yet established protection for different aspects of your life, you need to consult professionals to help you determine good solutions. Health and auto insurance are vital; property, life, disability and long-term care insurance will add to your peace of mind.

Step 5:
How to grow your assets? Do you have professionals to help you?

Congratulations if you have already completed the first four preliminary steps above.

In this step, you will think about ways to grow your assets so you can, at minimum, outpace inflation, minimize market risks, and strategically grow your assets.

At this point you need to understand basic financial principles, which is the purpose of this book. In addition, you will also want to find help from financial professionals, because they have more sophisticated knowledge and experience, as well as professional licenses to access the products and resources that the financial industry normally requires.

Different professionals have different expertise. You may need many of them working together for you, including financial planners, CPAs, insurance agents, estate planning lawyers, tax planners and asset management advisors. Some of these advisors can be from the same agency or from the same advisors who have expertise in several areas.

I have many friends who do not have experience with these kinds of financial professionals, usually because life is very busy. They are struggling to get to work, get their children to school and activities, and they simply don't have time to take care of everything. As a busy mom myself, I do not blame them, but I do want to emphasize the importance of getting access to these professionals to create current and future financial success for their families.

Nobody plans to fail, but they sometimes simply fail to plan. A family may spend days to plan a birthday party and weeks to plan a vacation; but they may not spend even a few hours to plan their family finances, which is one of the most important tasks to ensure a thriving life now and in the future.

Is it time to fit financial planning into your schedule and take action?

Step 6:
Have you thought about estate preservation?

When you are doing well financially, you might want to think about how much you want to leave to your children, grandchildren and future generations as your family legacy. You might also wish to support charitable causes you believe in.

Two things are important to know here: one is estate taxes and the other is how to build a family legacy using financial tools and strategies.

Think about this: if Donald Trump had not gotten his first seed money from his father, where he would be? He might be a middle-class worker like many others. It is very important to think beyond your own generation and consider your legacy to future generations.

Like me, many of you may also wish to support the mission of favored charities and give back to the community.

Some of you may feel this kind of planning is out of your league. But I am here to tell you that you do not need to be super rich to leave a decent legacy to future generations. Most middle-class families in this country have the capability to do so if they acquire the knowledge and get advice and assistance from the right professionals.

Needs at different life stages

We just dove into the six steps to clarify your financial needs. Next, we will look at special financial needs and things to watch out for at different ages and stages of life.

Age 30-40: Establishing proper protection

In general, most individuals and couples aged 30 to 40, with cars, kids, and a house, do not have many assets, but instead they have lots of liabilities. At this stage, establishing proper protection is critically important.

I know a couple who lived in Oakland, California. The husband was killed in a car accident, leaving behind a pregnant wife without much income. Because he did not have any protection planned, his wife and unborn child faced serious financial challenges.

Nobody is expecting to have a tragedy happen in their life, but proper protection ensures your family does not need to worry financially in case it happens. I hold the belief that having protection lowers the chance of tragedies, because the person subconsciously has peace of mind and he/she can be calmer in case of an emergency, which can sometimes create significantly different results.

And for people with children, the need to start planning for college funding is now, because the cost of higher education can be very high.

Age 40-50: Making a solid college plan

For many individuals/couples in this age range, assets have accumulated somewhat, but there is continued financial burden with the kids still at home. At this stage of life, families should accumulate assets, learn how to lower their taxes, and make a solid plan for college costs and future retirement.

Age 50-60: Planning for retirement

Many individuals/couples nearing retirement have grown children and are becoming more wealthy with less liability. There may be more or less financial burden depending on how the family was doing in the past 20 years.

Some families are doing financially well and have become financially independent. They do not need to rely on jobs or work for income to pay their living expenses. For these families, the important things to consider are:

a) Protecting assets from market risks
b) Saving on taxes
c) Regularly reviewing their retirement plans
d) Ensuring they have a plan for long-term care
e) Thinking about their legacy for future generations or causes

Some families may find themselves still working to make ends meet at this stage in their life. In this situation, try to lower expenses, continue to have insurance protection, and save as much as possible.

Age 60 and up: Estate planning

Individuals/couples at retirement age may still be able to work and make good income; however, if they have prepared well for retirement, they may prefer to only work at their own will.

Important considerations for retirement include lifetime income and insurance for long-term care, as 70% of people over age 65 need long-term care at some point.

Needs for retirement planning

The reality is you need to start saving for retirement as soon as you start generating income. We normally hear that the general rule is to save 10% of your income toward retirement. But how do you know how much you will need to spend when you retire and how much savings is enough??

Below are a few general rules.

In your 20s, start saving toward retirement from your first paycheck. Ten percent is a good rule of thumb.

In your 40s and 50s, you need to establish your retirement lifetime income that can cover your basic essentials such as housing, food, utilities, and transportation.

In your 60s, you need to have a solid plan for every aspect of your retirement income, including:

a) What retirement income you can expect from each account
b) The features of these accounts, including rate of return, risks, taxes, and liquidity
c) The different results in cash flow and account balance if you take retirement income from each account
d) The effects of common strategies, such as reverse mortgage, Roth conversion, 401(k) conversion to cash value life insurance

(CVLI) and annuities. How might each of these strategies affect your retirement?

When people think about retirement planning, they generally think about 401(k)s or similar plans provided by employers.

The financial industry evolves quickly, similar to technology industries. Be aware that there are multiple plans and newer products that can help you in your retirement planning beside 401(k)s, including annuities and cash value life insurance.

Annuities have tax-deferred growth and can provide lifetime income so you will never outlive your retirement income. The current trend is going to fixed indexed annuity, which removes stock market volatility and has good growth potential compared to its predecessors: fixed annuities and variable annuities.

A relatively newer type of permanent life insurance, sometimes called cash value life insurance (CVLI) can also be designed as an effective tool for retirement planning to establish a lifetime tax-free income.

2

Financial Concepts You Need to Know

American economist Ben Bernanke once said, "I don't think there are any students who should not be exposed to a basic financial literacy course." Most people in the United States have not received financial education, although this is one of the most important topics in our lives.

In order to achieve peace of mind in our personal finance, we need to understand a few very fundamental rules. You do not need to have the capability to analyze stock curves or read company financial reports. You just need to learn a few quick and simple concepts here that will lead you a long way toward financial literacy.

These concepts include:

1. The Rule of 72: The power of compound ing interest
2. Managing Risks: Analyzing different types of financial risks
3. Tax Structures: Categorizing different investment and savings options according to their tax features
4. Financial Foundation Layers: Three layers from lowest to highest that people need to consider in their personal finance
5. Diversification: Implementing a diverse set of strategies

1. The Rule of 72

Have you heard of the rule of 72? It is about the power of compound interest. Albert Einstein once said that compound interest is the most powerful force in the world.

The Rule of 72 tells you how many years it takes to double your money. For example, if the compound interest rate is 4%, it will take 18 years, which is calculated by dividing 72 by 4. For a compound interest rate of 8% it will take 9 years to double your money; at 12% it will take 6 years.

The table on the next page shows what happens when a 30-year-old invests $10,000.

AGE	4% Double in 18 years	8% Double in 9 years	12% Double in 6 years
30	$10,000	$10,000	$10,000
36 (+6 years)			$20,000
39 (+9 years)		$20,000	
42 (+12 years)			$40,000
48 (+18 years)	$20,000	$40,000	$80,000
54 (+24 years)			$160,000
57 (+27 years)		$80,000	
60 (+30 years)			$320,000
66 (+36 years)	$40,000	$160,000	$640,000

As you can see, the difference between compound interest rates is significant. It's the difference between having $40,000 at retirement or $640,000, making your retirement quite challenging or quite comfortable.

This teaches us two important things:

- The compound interest rate is so important to the ending result, and although the difference between a 4% and a 12% interest rate may not feel like a huge deal for some of us, when we understand the Rule of 72, we know how vital it is to find the best rate.

- Using different financial strategies in your personal finance can make a huge difference in your life.

At the time this book was written in early 2020 most banks were offering very low interest rates – from zero to two percent.

In comparison, the stock market annual growth is around 10%. A type of cash value life insurance (CVLI) has returns around 6% to 7%, or even more (up to 12%) with advanced features, with the additional benefits of being free of tax and no market risks.

In addition, most people know investing in real estate can be profitable. Historically, real estate investments net about 3.5% annually in the U.S.; some areas may have a much higher return, such as more than 5% in California. This return on investment can be greater if the mortgage is used, which means you borrow money to make money, and if the housing market growth outpaces the interest you pay. Investing in real estate does require consideration of other cost factors such as taxes and repairs and finding quality renters.

2. Managing Risks

Let's begin with a quick quiz:

Alice and Betty each have $100,000 to invest in the stock market.

In year one, Alice lost 50% of her investment due to market volatility (such as in 2009 when S&P dropped 40%+).

In year two, Alice gained 50%.

Betty was aware of the market risk and cashed out all her stock investment a year before 2009, therefore: In year one, Betty's investment stayed the same, 0% gain.

In year two, Betty's investment stayed the same again, 0% gain.

The question for you is which one you would like to be – Alice or Betty?

Say your answer out loud before you turn to the next page...

Most readers would like to become Alice, because she gained 50% in year two, which sounds pretty good. And it sounds very boring to be Betty, because it seems she is doing nothing or nothing has happened.

Let us calculate the results here:

For Alice:
In year one, she lost 50% of $100,000. She has $50,000 left.

In year two, she gained 50% of her remaining base, or $25,000 leaving her with $75,000.

For Betty:
In year one, she has $100,000.
In year two, she still has $100,000.

After this comparison you would rather be Betty, wouldn't you? It sounds counter intuitive, doesn't it?

What does this tell us?

It tells us that we need to be aware of the market risk. If you lose 50%, it takes 100% gain next year just to get back to where you began.

As Warren Buffet once said, the two most important rules for stock investment are:

1. Never lose money
2. Never forget rule number one

3. Tax Structures

There are two things nobody can avoid in this world, death and taxes.

There are so many taxes in our life. But for different types of savings and investment, there are three brackets in the tax structure:

Taxable

In this category, you need to pay tax for the capital gains. This category includes:

- Bank checking and savings accounts
- Brokerage accounts
- Bonds
- Real estate

Tax-Deferred

In this category you do not need to pay tax now, but you will be required to pay tax later for the capital gains. These types of structures are typically retirement related. The government encourages people to save for retirement, so it provides tax-deferred benefits to do so. This category includes:

- IRAs
- Sep/Simple IRAs
- 401(k) / 403(b) / 457 Plans
- Pensions
- Annuities

Tax-Advantaged

The capital gains of the funds in this category can be tax-exempt. This category includes:

- Roth IRAs
- Roth 401(k) / 403(b) Plans
- Municipal Bonds
- 529 Plans / Coverdell Plans
- Cash Value Life Insurance (CVLI)

The government provides tax advantages to the second and third categories because the government encourages people to save money for retirement, school tuition, or to protect themselves and their families with life insurance. Today, CVLI includes not only death benefits, but also living benefits, including long-term care, chronic and critical illness coverage, and safe saving tools for college funding and retirement income.

Most people are aware of taxable and tax-deferred categories, but may not be as familiar with tax-advantaged programs. This could be due to the fact that typically tax-advantaged programs have some restrictions and not everyone can qualify. There are also limits on how much you can save in these programs and how you can use the money. These are fairly sophisticated financial tools, and it is recommended that you work with trained specialists to help you understand them and set them up for you.

4. Financial Foundation Layers

To build a solid financial foundation for any person or family, we recommend three fundamental layers: the bottom layer is Protection; the middle layer is Lifetime Income, the top level is Lifestyle. Families need to start from bottom working their way up.

Protection Layer

The most basic financial foundation for every person or family is to make sure you cover the protection layer, which includes the protection of life, inflation, market risk, tax and health risks.

For example, if the main breadwinner of the house loses his or her life or becomes ill and cannot bring income home, the family may be in a harsh financial situation if he or she has not planned for any protection such as life insurance.

You should be aware of protecting your assets from market risk. Sharp swings in the market can wipe away the majority of your investments in a day.

You should also protect yourself from inflation. The average annual inflation rate in the USA is around 3% in the recent three decades. If you put all of your money into the bank with an almost 0% interest rate, you are actually losing 3% of your buying power every year, and over the course of 24 years, you could lose up to 50% of your buying power.

Lifetime Income Layer

When you are young and healthy, you can work and make income, so you can cover the basic fixed living expenses (housing, food, transportation, etc.) with your earnings. But when you are in retirement age, or if you get sick, you may no longer be able to work and generate income. You should have a plan that can bring in your lifetime income no matter how long you may live.

Statistics show that human beings are continuing to live longer and longer. The current life expectancy for women is 82 and for men it is 78. For couples, there is a 50% chance that one partner will live beyond 92 years and a 25% chance that one will live to 97. One of the worst things I can imagine is running out of money before you run out of life.

Nobody wants to be a burden on your children or be forced to rely on welfare in their golden years.

Where do you get lifetime income? How can you plan for it? There are many financial programs to help you and we will go deeper into them in later chapters.

Lifestyle Layer

After you have laid out a solid foundation for the first layer of protection, and then planned well for your lifetime income, you can consider some lifestyle costs and investments.

You may choose to invest your extra money into the stock market, into startup companies, crypto money, or any investment with higher risks.

Yes, there are some risks. You may lose your money partially or even fully, but you might gain a lot as well.

If you lose some money, it is not end of the world since you have already covered your basic and lifetime needs. You can still have peace of mind and live your life normally without becoming desperate.

If you gain well from your other investments, you may choose to spend your extra cash on shopping, travelling or any luxury dreams you may have. Or you may choose to contribute more to your favorite charities.

5. Diversification

"Do not put all of your eggs in one basket" is a golden rule in personal finance.

Different investment strategies have different features in aspects of tax structure, growth rate, market risks, liquidity, how safe the accounts are, the entry requirement, how much management is required, whether it can be used as collateral to borrow money, and additional benefits.

There are no good or bad accounts, but instead every investment account is unique with different features. What we need to do is to understand the different features of each investment strategy and use them wisely to accomplish our goals.

To be well diversified, you need to have lots of different kinds of investments. That means you should have some of each of the following: stocks, bonds, real estate (or funds), international securities, cash, and savings accounts without market risks.

Investments in each of these different asset categories do different things for you.

- Stocks help your portfolio grow
- Bonds bring in income
- Real estate provides both a hedge against inflation and low "correlation" to stocks—in other words, it may rise when stocks fall
- International investments provide growth and help maintain buying power in an increasingly globalized world
- Cash and savings accounts without market risks give you and your portfolio security and stability

How do you figure out how much money to put into each investment category?

First, set aside enough money in cash and income investments to handle emergencies and near-term goals.

Next, use the following rule of thumb: Subtract your age from 100 if you are a moderate risk taker (or 110 if you are a moderate to aggressive risk taker, or 120 if you are an aggressive investor) and put the resulting percentage in stocks; the rest in bonds.

In other words, if you prefer moderate risk, when you are 40 years old put 60% of your assets in stocks or other accounts which have growth potential but some market risks and put 40% in bonds or other accounts with little market risks.

Most 401(k) plans contain both stock and bond offerings; you can also buy these investments through an IRA.

3

Financial Tools

In this chapter, we will introduce common financial tools and products and their associated features in terms of rate of return, risks, liquidity, tax features and additional benefits.

Common financial tools and products in the U.S. are:

1) Bank accounts: Checking, Saving, CD, Money Market
2) Retirement accounts: 401(k)/403(b), IRA, Roth IRA, Annuity
3) Investment accounts: Mutual funds, ETFs, Stocks
4) Municipal bonds
5) 529 Plans

6) Cash Value Life Insurance: whole life, universal life, indexed universal life
7) Real estate investment
8) Other investment types

We will discuss the features of these tools and the typical applications and examples one by one.

1. Bank accounts: Checking, Savings, CD, Money Market

Most people are familiar with these common financial tools provided by banks. The money saved in a bank is generally considered "safe" because banks are protected by the Federal Deposit Insurance Corporation (FDIC).

In general, people do not need to worry about risks to their money in the bank, especially if you have a balance less than $250k, which is the amount covered by FDIC insurance.

At current time (2020), the interest rate for checking accounts is near 0%; interest for saving accounts is generally less than 1%; and interest rates for CDs or money market accounts is generally about 1-2%, floating according to the market.

As noted above, money saved in banks is generally safe, but the interest rates are very low and hardly beat the inflation rate, which is estimated around 2-3% over the past several decades. This means that you actually lose buying power for the money you save in bank accounts.

However, almost everyone has bank accounts and saves money in them.

Why?

Because it is a safe place and the money is liquid, which means you can get to your money almost immediately whenever you want to use it.

It is also a perfect place to save your emergency fund, so you can use the money when there are needs. But we do not need to save more than what we need for our emergency fund in the bank (generally 6 months of expenses), since those monies will lose buying power due to the low interest rate. For additional money we have available, we need to consider other financial tools.

2. Retirement accounts: 401(k)/403(b)/457, IRA, Roth IRA, Annuity

a) 401(k)/403(b)/457

This category of financial plans is for retirement planning purposes. These accounts have tax advantages provided by the government. By providing tax-deferred benefits, the U.S. government encourages its citizens to save for their own retirement.

Many employers provide 401(k) programs for their employees. For education, non-profit organizations, or government, they provide 403(b) programs or additional 457 programs.

All of these programs are tax-deferred, which means they are pre-tax money from your income, but you will be required to pay taxes when you take the retirement money at their designated retirement age.

The common misconception is that people normally think you will pay less tax when you retire since you will not work and will make less income. Actually, that depends on two factors.

One factor is that you may still remain in the same income bracket since the tax brackets have a wide range. For example, in 2019, one tax bracket included a range of $60k (from $20k to $80k per individual or $80k to $160k for married couples).

In addition, you may have few tax-deductible items when you retire, such as housing mortgage and child credits.

The second factor is the tax rate. We always feel the tax rate is high, but the current tax rate is relatively low when we look at the history of the past 90 years. The highest tax rate in 2018 is about 37%, and in comparison, it was 70% in 1980 for a couple with taxable income over $215k during President Jimmy Carter's time.

Currently, the U.S. federal government has over $23 Trillion in national debt which is historically at its highest, approximately the same amount of the GDP (Gross Domestic Production) of the country. The trend of the debt is increasing year after year. Just during President Barack Obama's time, the national deficit nearly doubled, from $11 Trillion at the beginning of his presidency to $20 Trillion at the end of his presidency.

What will government have to do in order to lower the national deficit? Experts say that increasing taxes in the future is the only way.

If we do not make significantly less money when we are at our retirement age and we have fewer tax deductions, we may experience higher tax rates.

Do you think you will end up paying more or less for your 401(k)/403(b)/457 money? Many professionals believe that middle class families may end up paying more taxes in retirement age.

Here is an example:

Jennifer and Jack are a middle-class couple in their 40s. Jack makes $80k and Jennifer makes $100k annually. They put $30k every year into their 401(k) plans. Their major tax-deductible item is the interest on their house mortgage - they are paying about $20k in interest annually now. They also have two kids for whom they can get tax credits.

The house has a 30-year mortgage. They bought it in their 30s and plan to pay it off in their 60s. When they retire at 67, they expect to have about $60k in annual income from social security, $80k from their retirement account, and they have income around $40k/year from their mutual fund investment which totals $180k. However, when they retire, they will not have their 401(k) contribution, tax credit for kids or house loan interest that could be counted as deductibles. In addition, there is a good chance that the tax rate will go up after 20 years.

As you can see for this couple, the taxes at their retirement could well be more than what they are paying now.

As shown in the above example for middle class families, if they are saving for retirement, have basic finance knowledge, and are doing generally well, they still have a good chance of paying more income tax during their retirement than they are paying now.

b) IRA

IRA stands for individual retirement account. A typical American works an average of twelve jobs in their lifetime, so they may have many 401(k) or other retirement accounts. It is generally a good practice to consolidate these accounts into one IRA account for the reasons below:

- It is easier to manage one IRA account than many different 401(k)/403(b) accounts
- In general, there are more investment choices in an IRA account than in an employer 401(k) account
- IRA has some advantages over 401(k)/403(b)

For example, when a person dies, if his or her money is in a 401(k), his or her beneficiaries have to take all the money out at once, which will be counted as one-time income and may result in a higher tax bracket.

If his or her money is in IRA, the beneficiaries can set up a plan to take a portion of the money out each year, which may result in less overall tax.

c) Roth IRA

Roth IRA is another type of retirement plan. The main difference between Roth IRA and traditional IRA (including 401(k), 403(b), 457) is its tax features.

Roth contributions are made with after-tax money, but the gains in the account do not need to be taxed again in the future. This is opposite to the traditional IRA, where the contribution is before-tax money, but future withdrawals are subject to taxes.

There is a maximum annual contribution of $5500 (in 2018) and there is also an income requirement. For example, a married couple must have a modified adjusted gross income of less than $199k. Many families in California are not eligible for contributing to the Roth IRA because their family income is higher than this amount, although they may convert their traditional IRA into a Roth IRA by paying the taxes..

Roth IRA has extraordinary tax benefits by paying no tax on gains in the account. Compared to the traditional IRA, it eliminates the risks of tax rate increase in the future. However, it may not be eligible for some families with higher incomes.

One alternative plan is cash value life insurance (CVLI), which is similar to Roth IRA and many families have used it to get the tax exemption benefits. However, it also has limitations, like all the other plans with government granted tax benefits, which will be discussed later in this chapter.

d) Annuity

Annuity is another type of retirement plan, which is tax deferred as well. You can think of this as a pension, since it provides guaranteed lifetime income if you choose the lifetime income feature.

You can roll over your 401(k) or other IRA account funds into an annuity or you can use your cash to fund an annuity account.

The biggest advantage of annuities is that the capital gain from an annuity account is tax-deferred and it does not have contribution limits, compared to your other retirement plans, such as 401(k).

3. Investment accounts: Mutual funds, ETFs, Individual Stocks

A mutual fund is a professionally managed investment fund that pools money from institutional investors and retail investors to purchase securities.

An exchange-traded fund (ETF) is an investment fund traded on stock exchanges, much like stocks, but it holds assets of stocks, commodities, or bonds. An ETF is traded as stocks.

Mutual funds and ETFs have a lot of similarities. Compared to investing directly in individual stocks, mutual funds and ETFs have advantages of a higher level of diversification, liquidity, and tax benefits since people do not need to trade as frequently as with individual stocks.

Mutual funds and ETFs have differences in minimum investment amount, trading time, and automatic operations.

Mutual funds and ETFs are professionally managed, and they are generally associated with various fees and expenses.

The management fee for ETFs or mutual funds is typically between 0.5% and 1.5% for actively managed funds, and 0-0.3% for passively managed funds.

Warren Buffet recommends investing in indexed mutual funds over actively managed funds or individual stocks, knowing that only about eight percent of mutual funds outperform S&P 500 index funds.

4. Municipal bonds

Municipal bonds are loans investors make to local governments. They are issued by cities, states, counties, or other local governments. For that reason, the interest they pay on the bonds is tax-free.

Most people buy municipal bonds through their financial advisor, bank, or even the municipality directly. Many people also benefit from purchasing municipal bonds through a bond fund.

Municipal bonds are generally very safe, similar to savings in a bank. Over the past 30 years, the average return has stayed steady around 5%.

5. 529 Plan for education

A 529 plan is a tax-advantaged savings account designed to be used for the beneficiary's education expenses. The money invested into a 529 plan is after-income tax money, which is different from 401(k) retirement plans. However, the capital gains and distributions are tax-free.

The stated purpose of a 529 fund is that the monies be used for education; you may receive a 10% penalty and have to pay federal taxes if you use it for other purposes.

Note, the 529 plan will be counted as the parents' investment asset when the student applies for college financial aid. Due to the potential penalties listed above if the fund is not used for education, many parents look into other ways to save for college funding.

6. Cash Value Life Insurance (CVLI)

Similar to cell phones, life insurance programs have evolved over the past decades. Here we will discuss term insurance, and several types of permanent insurance, which are also called cash value life insurance, including whole life, universal life and indexed universal life.

Most companies provide term insurance for their employees. The term generally is 10, 20 or 30 years. There is no cash value and no tax benefits in this plan. It only pays if the insured person dies during the term of the policy.

However, most people are young and healthy when they start term insurance, so there is very little chance that their families will actually get that benefit before the term expires.

Another type of life insurance is whole life insurance, which is a type of permanent life insurance. The premium is first applied to the cost of the insurance and the rest of the fund goes into savings which normally has a 3-4% annual growth. The capital gain in whole life is also generally tax-free if you are guided properly by professionals.

Variable universal life insurance is a type of cash value life insurance where the cash value can be invested in a wide variety of separate accounts similar to mutual funds with competitive annual growth. Like risks associated with mutual funds and stocks, universal life insurance may lose money when the market drops.

Most people who purchase permanent insurance do not like to take any market risks. People also want to have living benefits in addition to death benefits so they can cover their expenses in case they have a chronic or critical illness. To meet the growing and evolving needs of customers, many life insurance companies have developed a new type of permanent insurance called indexed universal life which provides living benefits in addition to death benefits for beneficiaries.

Indexed universal life insurance generates good cash value if it is designed properly. It also removes market risks. Generally, this type of product has a floor and a cap. If the stock market drops, you do not lose any money (that's the floor). If the stock market grows, you get growth potential (the cap). The cap is generally from 8% to 15% depending on different providers and different index strategies.

For example, if the market dropped 30%, the cash account in this policy will drop 0% and the insured does not lose money. When the market grows 8%, assuming the cap is 15%, the account will increase 8%. If the market grows 18%, the account will grow by the cap of 15%.

Historically, the average annual compound interest rate is from 5-10%; indexed universal life insurance can be tax-free if managed properly.

Compared to normal stock market investments, indexed universal life insurance eliminates market risks and it has a pretty good growth rate. In contrast, skillful stock investors who are comfortable with taking higher risks may get quick and much higher returns if they choose the right stocks at the right time.

Additionally, indexed universal life insurance can be a good tool to provide the fundamental protection layer and lifetime income layer, as well as college funding. A strategy called participating loan can generate steady and high retirement income if designed properly. Most people are not familiar with this type of life insurance, however, and it can be complicated to design and manage, requiring the services of an experienced financial professional with advanced insurance training.

I know that it can be difficult to understand the ins and outs of these products. My recommendation is that you seek out highly qualified professionals to help you understand and manage your funds in the most beneficial way. Again, like our modern cell phones, we might not understand exactly how they work but we know to choose a well-reviewed and well-respected brand.

7. Real estate investment

Real estate investment has been popular for many decades; it has made many people a fortune and, unfortunately, it has bankrupted others. Many people prefer to put their money into real estate, favoring this type of investment over other investment products and tools. They seek those potential fortunes as property values skyrocket, but they often fail to see the very real market risks, such as the housing market crash in 2008 (for example, according to the Federal Reserve Bank of St. Louis, the home price index in San Francisco in 2007 was 215 and by March, 2008 it had dropped almost 44% to 121). Overall, barring significant increases and drops in property values, long term real estate growth in the U.S. mirrors the inflation rate at about 3.5%, although there are some geographical areas that routinely outperform this national average.

Real estate investors also often fail to figure in the time and money costs of rental management, repair, and maintenance. Average net rental income is about 3 to 5% of the total investment after paying the property taxes, renters' insurance, homeowner association fees, maintenance and repair fees, and property management costs.

As you will read in case studies shared later in this book, we have seen both winning stories and losing stories in real estate investment. I have seen many people lose their investment homes and their assets accumulated over decades in the volatile housing market, so I want to caution readers to be vigilant about the risks involved.

There are many other investment strategies that bring a greater return with less challenges, such as fixed income funds or indexed universal life insurance with a lifetime income solution.

Mr. Teddy Fang, an experienced financial advisor, provides a thoughtful example here:

Tony, a 47-year-old male would like to consider options to invest $1M cash for his retirement. He wants to retire at age 60.

Option A: Invest in real estate now. In 13 years when Tony reaches age 60, the real estate value is estimated at about $1.5 Million. The after-cost and after-tax income from this investment is about 3% to 5% of the $1.5 Million, which is about $45k to $75k annually.

Option B: Save the money in an indexed universal life insurance fund. Depending on the provider and strategy used, the annual income in 13 years will be between $60k and $200k tax-free, with the added peace of mind of having life insurance and living benefits in case of illness.

Option C: Invest money in high-yield mutual funds, such as SRET (SuperDividend REIT ETF). This fund was started in 2015 and is pretty new, but the yield is as high as 6-8% compared to the average of 4% to 6% for 401(k) plans or standard mutual funds. In 13 years when Tony retires, this asset can have doubled to $2M resulting in annual retirement income of $80k to $120k before taxes. The potential drawback: there are always market risks in this type of investment.

So, looking at options A, B and C, what should Tony do? Most people would choose B wouldn't they?

If Tony were asking for my guidance, I would remind him of the vital importance of diversification, allowing for some riskier investments with high growth potential, and others with more steady outcomes. I would suggest three types of investment portfolios with investments about equally distributed.

8. Other Investment Types: Business Investment, Angel Fund, Venture Capital Fund, Cryptocurrency

There are multiple other ways to invest money. Many people have interests in business. They may invest in restaurants, retail stores and myriad other businesses.

The general advice would be if you want to invest in any business, you should become an expert in that industry so you have your best chance to invest wisely.

Many people invest in startup companies by being part of the angel fund or being a limited partner of venture capital. These forms are highly risky. I would suggest only investing an amount that will not change your lifestyle should you lose this investment.

Cryptocurrency is very recent phenomenon. Cryptocurrencies are a kind of digital currency using decentralized control. Many people went in early and have already made a fortune. Latecomers may still have a chance to make money, but there is a high risk of losing your investment.

Let's look at Bitcoin as an example. Bitcoin is a new concept and is considered very risky:

- Price was less than $100 in July, 2013
- Price rose to nearly $1,000 in January, 2014
- Price peaked at $19,000 in December, 2017
- Price then dropped quickly to around $6,000 in November, 2018

For those wishing to get into this volatile investment area, I would suggest using less than 1% of your total available assets as you learn about this area. This way you will not lose out on a potential good opportunity but will also not jeopardize a significant amount of your assets. If you identify a new opportunity early, say you bought into Bitcoin in 2014 at $1000 and sold in 2017 at $15,000, you would have made 15 times your investment in just three years. But, if you entered late in 2017, you would have lost two-thirds of your investment in just one year. It's a gamble.

9. Quick Comparison of Different Tools

We have discussed the common investment methods and highlighted their features. We will list them below for a quick comparison in terms of annual returns, market, tax categories (taxable, tax-deferred, tax-advantaged), liquidity (how quickly you can access your money) and their typical usage.

People may use some or all of these investment tools to meet their financial needs and goals.

Bank savings: Annual return of 0-2%, no market risk, taxable, very liquid, good for emergency fund

Retirement accounts invested in mutual funds, ETFs and stocks: Average return of 6-8% in the long term, very high market risks, tax deferred, not liquid before 59.5 years old, good for retirement fund

Retirement accounts in annuities, assuming fixed index annuity: Annual growth of 5-8% in long term, no market risks, guaranteed lifetime income, tax deferred, not liquid before age 59.5, good for retirement fund

Brokerage accounts in mutual funds, ETFs and stocks: Annual returns can be negative to very high depending on the picks, with the average return for the market from 5-10% in the long term, very high market risks, taxable, a common part of a wealth accumulation portfolio

NOTE: These accounts sound very liquid but in fact may not be since most investors are not leaning to sell stocks when it is a bull market (on the rise), thinking the stocks could go even higher and they might miss out on a greater return.

Municipal bonds: Average return of 3-5% in the long term, little market risk, tax advantaged, liquid or not depending on the terms of the bonds, a conservative investment method and an essential part of entire wealth accumulation portfolio

529 plans: Average return around 5%, medium market risk, tax advantaged, less liquid since it can be only used for education purposes, can be used for preparing educational fund

NOTE: The funds in this plan will be accounted as personal assets on the college financial aid forms.

Cash Value Life Insurance (CVLI): Whole life insurance: Average return is 3-5% for the savings, no market risks, tax advantaged, not very liquid

Universal life: Average return of 6-8% for the savings, market risks, tax advantaged, liquid

Indexed universal life insurance: Average return of 6-8% for the savings, no market risks, tax advantaged, liquid

Real estate: Average return of 3-4% for home price increase over a long term, 3-5% for after-tax net rental income, some market risks, taxable

NOTE: Real estate investment is not easily liquid. The only way you can take a large amount of funds out is through a line of credit, refinancing or selling the property. There are strict criteria for lines of credit and refinancing regarding income, assets, credit scores and loan amount, which may restrict access to funds in an urgent situation.

Business or private funds or other forms of investment: Average returns can be from negative to very high, very high market risks, taxable

NOTE: Depending on different situations, this type of investment can be liquid or not. These forms of investments are used by a relatively small number of people who understand unique forms of investment.

4

Identify Your Spending Style

People fall into one of three categories according to their spending styles: debtors, savers, and wealth creators. Which category are you in? Is this how you want to manage your finances?

Debtors

Debtors spend more than they make, so they are in debt. After they receive income, they need to spend a portion to pay back the debt, thus limiting the funds they have for saving and for their regular expenses. Their life is often stressful since their finances are usually under water.

They generally pay high interest rates for their debts, such as credit card debt. In general, if the person does not have good assets as collateral, and/or a high credit rating, it is difficult for them to borrow money with a good interest rate. They may even struggle to find financial institutions that are willing to lend them money.

Remember, not all debts are bad. We call the ones with high interest rates bad debt. As a quick rule of thumb, if the interest rate is higher than 8%, you should try to avoid it.

NOTE: Interest rates vary at different times and are related to many factors, such as the current inflation rate. In this decade, the inflation rate is relatively low, from 1-3%. In this environment, an interest rate of 8% is pretty high.

There are some good debts, however, such as home mortgage debts. Home mortgage interest rates are generally 2-5% for a 30-year fixed term, and the value of the home usually appreciates over time. In addition, this debt is tax deductible so it can help to grow a family asset over time.

What about student loans? It depends. Some student loans have a zero percent interest rate when the student is at school and some have a very low interest rate, such as a Strafford unsubsidized student loan, which is around 4%, so we would consider these as good debts. But some carry much higher interest rates up to 7% or more. For these loans, students and parents need to be very careful.

The most important goals for debtors:

1. Face your financial situation and take control
2. Eliminate bad debts with high interest
3. Reign in spending and/or increase income
4. Begin saving a minimum of 10% of your income
5. Grow assets and learn how to make your money work for you

By consistently prioritizing these goals you will begin to feel less overwhelmed, more in control, and more fulfilled in life.

Savers

Savers have established the good habit of saving a portion of their income. I've been a saver since childhood, having learned this habit from my parents. They always saved 20% of their income no matter how little they made and stayed within the budget they had. I naturally adopted this outlook and began saving with my very first earnings – a small scholarship I received for college back in the early 1990s.

Savers typically have lower financial stress when compared with debtors. However, many savers are so debt averse that they choose to pay for large ticket items, including vehicles, college costs and even homes, with cash, and thus deplete their savings and the growth those dollars can return.

Savers often think that any debt is bad debt. Their logic is to avoid paying interest on loans by paying cash for the item. This makes sense for smaller ticket items, but it may work against you in the long run.

Here is a perfect example. Say Tom pays cash for a new car instead of financing that purchase. The car is $40,000 and Tom pulls that money from his savings. If he were to finance the purchase at 2% interest for 5 years, his monthly payment would be $701 and the total interest paid in 5 years would be $2,067. If he put his $40,000 in an indexed account at 6% growth each year, he would earn $13,954 – that's a net of $11,887 after deducting the $2,067 in interest for the loan. And, he always has access to the $40,000 capital – it is not tied up in a quickly depreciating vehicle.

Traditional wisdom teaches people to be savers. Good savings habits build a good personal finance foundation. I want to teach savers how to take the next step to become wealth creators so they can make their money work for them and create long-term security for their families.

Wealth Creators

Wealth creators have created a solid financial foundation and have made the leap from simply saving to making their money work for them. They know when to pay for purchases with cash and when to finance purchases at good interest rates. They know how to make their money grow at the highest rates of return. Over time, this makes a huge difference in their financial outlook.

Once I learned how to think strategically about my assets and how they can create bigger benefits, I made the transition myself, from being a conscientious saver to being a creator of wealth.

The car loan example above illustrates how wealth creators think. By investing their $40,000 well and taking a low interest loan for the vehicle, the wealth creator ends up with more than $11,000 over the 5 years of the loan while maintaining control of those dollars. Having that money available instead of invested in a car can be very important in case of the loss of a job or other financial struggle.

A couple came to me last year seeking my advice on their financial situation. The couple has three children in middle school and high school. Both the wife and husband had recently lost their consulting jobs and the good income they relied on. Before their layoffs, they had managed to pay off their home, valued close to a million dollars. But they had very little in their savings or other liquid accounts. Their first solution was to refinance their house to take out some cash, but their request was denied because they could not show current sources of income.

Basically, all of their assets were tied up in their house and they had little to cover their day-to-day expenses. They had only two options. Find new jobs quickly, or sell the house, which could take a significant amount of time and could result in a loss on their investment.

If they hadn't moved so quickly to pay off their house and instead invested half of the value ($500,000) in brokerage or other liquid accounts, they could have stayed in their home and lived with much less stress while they looked for new sources of income.

Even when you are doing well, you should always make risk management plans in case of a financial downturn. Wealth creators are wise to include smart management of liquid assets in their financial strategy.

What have we learned from the three spending styles?

If you are a debtor, budget your expenses and set up goals to save at least 10% of your income and pay off your bad debts.

If you are a saver, make smart decisions about taking loans or paying with cash for big purchases and learn how to make your money work for you and bring greater returns in the long run.

If you are already a wealth creator, congratulations! Keep doing what you are doing to manage risk and create additional wealth.

5

What is Financial Freedom?

(And How Can You Get There?)

You can achieve peace of mind in your personal finances before you become financially free. However, true financial freedom is the key to true peace.

What is the definition of financial freedom?

Financial freedom means different things for different people.

To some people, financial freedom means having the ability to choose your dream work without worrying about the paycheck. For others, it is the ability to pay for their children's college education. Still others see financial freedom as the ability to make their travel and adventure dreams come true. For most of us, financial freedom means being able to retire when you want to and maintain your desired lifestyle without a paycheck.

In all of these instances, we rely on our passive income to safely cover our expenses. Passive income is not the income from active work; rather it is generated from passive activities such as investment of stocks, rental homes, businesses, etc.

The following steps can help you determine what financial freedom means to you and how you can get there.

1. Figure out the cost of your desired lifestyle

Rebecca and her husband, Grant, are in their mid-40s and have two kids, ages 11 and 14. Both are well educated and work for large corporations. They currently live comfortably in a suburb of New York City, one of the most expensive areas in the world. They own a single-family, 4 bedroom, two-story home built in 2010. They love their Italian-styled community featuring well designed and maintained landscaping and public sculpture installations.

Luckily, they bought the house at the low market point in 2010 during the economic downturn caused by housing bubbles and the credit crisis. The house cost $800k. With a 20% down payment and a low interest rate, their monthly mortgage is about $3200.

They are very happy with their local public school system, but, like many middle-class families, they have other expenses related to their kids' interests and activities including private coaches and programs. Their kids are involved in ice skating, soccer, swimming, springboard diving, martial arts, golfing, gymnastics, tumbling and trampoline, dancing, track and field, tennis, piano, flute, clarinet, art, speaking and debate, writing, summer camps, and leadership programs. The family is also working with college planning consultants. Their monthly outlay for all of these activities runs to $1,000 or more.

The kids enjoy these activities and they have helped to build their confidence and their academic success. Like most parents, Rebecca and Grant see these expenses as an appropriate investment in their kids and their futures.

Other costs for this family are regular living expenses, such as their car loan, insurance, maintenance, and gas; travelling and entertainment; utilities; internet and phones; food; clothing; and other miscellaneous expenses. They also pay for medical insurance through a plan offered by an employer and take advantage of a 401(k) savings plan.

Above that, their other major costs are cash value life insurance policies. They found these programs are very useful for middle-class families like theirs, since these policies provide protection, tax benefits, no-risk and potentially high return rates. Each member of the family has a $1.5-million cash value life insurance policy, including the kids. The targeted premiums for these policies add up to about $3,000 per month.

They also own a number of rental homes and their current rental income covers the mortgages, meaning these costs do not need to be considered in their monthly expenses.

This is their monthly expense breakdown*:

House Mortgage: (including property tax and insurance)	$3,200
Car payment, insurance, maintenance:	$800
Kids' activities:	$1,000
Utilities, internet, cell phones:	$300
Food/Clothing:	$2,000
Entertainment/Travel:	$1,000
Charity & Gifts:	$400
Misc.:	$500
Employer Sponsored Health Insurance:	$300
401(k):	$500
Cash value life insurance: (protection & investment)	$3000
TOTAL (without cash value life insurance)	$10,000
TOTAL (with cash value life insurance)	$13,000

As we see above, this family's minimum expenses will be around $10k/month or $120k per year, not considering the cash value life insurance, which is meant for long-term investment and family legacy.

*Note, these numbers are rounded to make it easy for calculation.

2. Calculate how much you need invested to generate enough passive income to cover the cost of your desired lifestyle

In this step, you will calculate the financial assets you need in order to generate the passive income required to cover your anticipated expenses.

Rebecca's family is a typical middle-class family living in an expensive area. Their lifestyle is comfortable but not luxurious.

Both Rebecca and her husband work for large corporations and have stable income and benefits. For the past eight years, their family income has been well above $200k annually. In addition, they began saving and investing 15 years ago and have accumulated some wealth.

In step one we calculated that Rebecca's family needs $120k after-tax passive income annually. So, we need to consider the implication of taxes next.

Most of their investments are in the form of stocks, mutual funds, bonds, and their rental properties, all of which are taxable. Rebecca and Grant also have savings and investment in cash-value life insurance (CVLI), which do not require them to pay capital gains taxes. Between all of their investments, we assume an average taxation of 20%.

Let us calculate:

They need $120k of after-tax income. They will be taxed up to 20% on their investments. Which means they will need to generate $150k in before-tax income.

If the average annual investment return is 5%:
They will need $3M in assets (5% of $3M = $150K).

If the average annual investment return is 7.5%:
They will need $2M in assets (7.5% of $2M = $150k).

If the average annual investment return is 10%:
They will need $1.5M in assets (10% of $1.5M = $150k).

If the average annual investment return is 15%:
They will need $1M in assets (15% of $1M = $150k).

In the past 65 years, the average S&P 500 growth rate is 10.35%. So, it would seem reasonable to expect to get this return rate. But I would like to warn you here, up to 90% of investors do not experience this rate of growth.

When a friend told me that his annual investment return was over 30%, I challenged him. We dug into 15 years of his investments and analyzed the results together. We found that the return on his stock investments averaged just 6%, far below the 30% he had estimated. Like many investors, he hadn't actually calculated the return on all of the assets in his portfolio.

But do not feel too bad about yourself if you find your investment return is much less than the S&P 500.

Why?

Ninety percent of professional fund portfolio managers cannot beat the S&P 500 in their results, according to the statistics. Think about that - these are trained professionals with full-time work experience and support from many analysts. As a non-professional, part-time investor, you do not have the extensive resources they have, so it would be hard to beat their performance.

We need to be knowledgeable and realistic in estimating our passive income, so we do not come up short to cover our needs.

The first step is to conduct a thorough analysis to determine the current return rate on your investments.

This is best done with the help of a financial professional.

Step two is to calculate how much in assets you need in order to generate the annual income you want. In Rebecca and Grant's case, that is $150k. They will need $3M in investments at a 5% return rate to generate that amount. But, if they can improve their return percentage to 10%, they would need just $1.5M to experience that financial freedom.

Improving your investment return to 10% brings financial freedom within reach. And a 10% return is realistic, as it is the average over the past 65 years.

Consider: many families do not live in such an expensive urban area, so the income you need from your investments may be much less than that needed by Rebecca and Grant.

For example, Jean and Jeremy have two kids and live comfortably in New Orleans, with living expenses at about $6k per month, or $72k annually. Jean's salary covers their living expenses, so they are able to save and invest Jeremy's income.

Using the assumptions above, if they get a 5% return on their investments, they would need to have $1.4M invested to generate the $72k they need for living expenses annually. Currently, they have $1.5M in their investments, so they have already achieved financial freedom.

We have simplified many details to make these calculations easy to understand We have not considered inflation, which can create a higher cost of living. We also have not considered any potential impact to your benefits, including health insurance, if you change employers.

3. Consider liquidity

One thing we need to address is the need for your assets (as calculated above) to be liquid if you are relying on that income to cover your living expenses.

Let's look again at the example of Rebecca and Grant. If they were both to quit (or lose) their corporate jobs today, and had no source of income, they would need access to $120k right away to cover their current and on-going living expenses. As we calculated above, at a return of 5%, they would need to have $3M in investment assets to create the liquid funds they can access as they need. If those assets are in retirement accounts such as a 401(k) or in real estate holdings, the gains they anticipate would not be available in liquid form to access as needed.

Types of investments that create liquid and accessible income include stocks, mutual funds, ETFs, savings in bank accounts, and well-designed cash value life insurance (CVLI).

There are many funds with consistently good dividends. One such fund is Vanguard High Dividend

Yield Index Fund (VHDYX), with yearly dividends around 3%. This is a good performance fund, with the price tripled from September, 2008, to July, 2018, even with such high dividend payout. This fund's 10-year performance (2008-2018) is 10.12% pre-tax.

Investing in S&P 500 funds is a good choice as well. These funds mirror index holdings and generally charge low fees. For example, Fidelity Spartan 500 Index (FUSEX) has an expense ratio of 0.1% and their 10-year performance is 10.09%.

Cash value life insurance (CVLI) can be a good choice to generate liquid income if it is designed well. As an example, Mary has been saving and investing using CVLI since she began her career at age 25. She has always invested the annual maximum of $17k and by the time she is 50, the account has a face value of $1M. If she were to begin taking annual income from this account, she would receive between $50k and $100k, depending on which programs and strategies she selected. Another positive for this type of investment is that the capital gains from the account are generally tax-free.

4. Improve your investments

Once we have calculated the annual income needed to support our desired lifestyle and determined the amount of investment assets required to meet that annual income, we need to learn how to manage our finances well, so we can reach financial freedom early and safely.

The key here is to improve your investment returns without significantly increasing investment risks.

There are many things you can do to become financially savvy and improve your investment mindset and skills. Reading this book is a great start. You may choose to meet with or follow a few good financial professionals to learn how to make your money work for you. There are trainings you can take, and you may want to join an investment club with a circle of money-savvy members you can learn from. Getting smarter about your money can create significant improvements on your returns. Investing your time in learning how to improve your investments can make the difference between financial struggle and financial freedom.

Let us quickly calculate how much more return you can get by improving your investment strategies.

These calculations illustrate a scenario of a 45-year-old investor with $1M in assets.

In 20 years, when you are 65:

a) If your average annual after-tax investment return is 0.01% (such as the rate you may get from checking or bank savings accounts) your asset will become $1.002M.

Calculation: $1M x (1+0.01%) ^ 20 = $1.002M

b) If your average after-tax annual investment return is 1% (such as the rate you may get from CDs in the bank), your asset will become $1.22M.

Calculation: $1M x (1+1%) ^ 20 = $1.22M

c) If your average after-tax annual investment return is 3% (such as the rate you may get from government bonds), your asset will become $1.81M.

Calculation: $1M x (1+3%) ^ 20 = $1.81M

d) If your average after-tax annual investment return is 4% (such as the rate you may get from a 529 college plan), your asset will become $2.19M.

Calculation: $1M x (1+4%) ^ 20 = $2.19M

e) If your average after-tax annual investment return is 6% (such as the rate you may get from a brokerage account), your asset will become $3.21M.

Calculation: $1M x (1+6%) ^ 20 = $3.21M

f) If your average annual investment return is 7%, your asset will become $3.87M.

Calculation: $1M x (1+7%) ^ 20 = 3.87M

If you read this book, apply what you learn, and/or get help from professionals, it is not difficult at all to improve your return modestly by a couple of percentage points, making a significant difference in your wealth over 20 years or longer.

If your current annual return is 3%, and you apply what you have learned to invest more strategically, you could increase that return to 7% without increasing your risks. In the scenario above that would improve your total net assets from $1.8M to $3.8M – and that is a lot of money!

5. A true story and what we can learn from it

I know two families: the Richardsons and the DeWitts. Both couples are of similar age, with similar age kids, similar incomes, and similar lifestyle costs. Both couples are conscientious savers and for the past 15 years they have put the maximum allowed into their 401(k) plans.

When I compared their 401(k) accounts, I was shocked. The DeWitt family has amassed about $900k and the Richardsons have only $350k. The difference is over half a million dollars!

I began an investigation to figure out why. What I found was a big difference in how they managed their assets since the market crash in 2008. Like everyone else, both families lost a big chunk of money in their accounts when the market dropped almost 50%. The DeWitts kept all of their investment portfolio untouched (which means they left their money in their accounts and did not make changes). They decided to ride it out, thinking that when the market comes back, they will gain back what was lost and then their money would keep increasing.

The Richardsons got really nervous when the market took such a big dip and they sold almost all of their mutual funds, ETFs and other stocks in their accounts and kept them in the cash account in their 401(k). When the market came back over the following years, they missed the opportunity to catch up and were not able to take advantage of the power of compound interest. While we can understand being nervous, their strategy ended up losing them almost $500,000 - money that could have made the difference in them reaching financial freedom and building wealth for the future.

Many families like the Richardsons never understand the magnitude of their financial loss because they are simply unaware of it. They don't know what they don't know.

Why is this? In our society, we tend to keep our finances strictly confidential and we don't have ways for family members and friends to share, compare and learn from one another.

I believe in the power of sharing, discussing, and learning from each other.

It is one of the goals of this book to share real stories from real people around us, so you can think, compare, explore, and benefit from them. I salute our generous contributors who shared their stories, their joys and pains, and their lessons learned so we can all get better at managing our finances and understanding how financial freedom is created.

There is one more thing for you to ponder. If one mistake could cause you to forfeit half a million dollar or more, the flip side is also true: one successful tactic could help you gain millions of dollars. I hope that you will avoid such costly mistakes and learn successful investment strategies by:

1. Making time to learn from this book
2. Applying the strategies shared here and your newfound knowledge of personal finances with the help of savvy financial professionals
3. Registering online at DrSherryHu.com to take advantage of the free online tools and resources I have available to help you get on the road to financial freedom

6

Case Studies of Real People

The secret for improving in any area is to learn not just from your own experiences and mistakes, but from other people's as well.

In this chapter, we will share real life stories of a few financially wise women. We will learn from their experiences.

Case 1: Susan, a woman who believes in exploring and getting professional help in personal finance

Susan and her husband were in their early 30s with two young children. They both had stable jobs and income and had started to accumulate financial assets thanks to their good habit of saving. They began exploring investing in real estate and the stock market to make their money work for them.

They entered into real estate investing by purchasing three homes in Las Vegas in 2005, 2007 and 2008. During that period, the housing market in the United States peaked in 2006 and dropped sharply in 2009. Locally, the highs and lows in Las Vegas were even more dramatic and home prices in 2010 dropped 66% compared to 2006. They began to rise in 2012.

Project 1

In Susan's first home investment project in 2005, they bought a home for around $300k with a 20% down payment. In 2010, this house was valued at just $120k. They rented this house out and it was occupied the entire time, but the rental income did not fully cover their mortgage, so they had to cover the balance from their own budget. Since this investment was actually costing them money, not to mention the cost of repairs and upkeep and the trouble they had dealing with renters, they decided to sell in 2017 when the value rose to $240k – a loss of $60k on the original purchase price.

For this real estate investment project, the end result is that they lost roughly $60k (20% of the purchase price).

Project 2

In 2008, when the market had a big drop, Susan and her husband bought another home in Las Vegas for $230k which was about 60% of the price the previous owner paid in 2005.

For this rental home, they put down 25%, which was $57.5k. They were concerned about this investment as they watched the housing market continue to drop. In 2012 the house was valued at just $160k. Finally, the market began to climb, and they sold the house in 2019 for $330k (netting them $310k after transaction fees). They made the decision to sell because the market was volatile, and they thought values might begin to drop again.

The rough return for this investment project of 11 years: ROI = 139% calculated from (310 – 230)/57.5. The annualized ROI = 8.2%.

Note: This is a simplification as we did not detail costs of repairs, taxes, etc.

Susan and her husband learned a few important things from their experiences in real estate investment:

- Always be aware of housing market risks
- Timing is critically important for real estate investment
- Location is critical too - housing markets across the U.S. and internationally are unique and experience local value trends

- Real estate investment includes many considerations such as property taxes, home association fees, repair and maintenance costs, income taxes, and getting and keeping renters

In general, rental income averages around 3-5% of the market price of the property after considering all the above factors. For example, if you bought a $500k home in California, the net rental income after all the costs and taxes is around $15k to $25k annually.

New phase

It is now 2020 and Susan is in her mid-40s. Her career has continued to advance, and she is thinking about making some changes to chase her life's dream. Her children will be off to college in a few years. She and her husband want to have a solid financial plan for their kids' education as well as security for their retirement in the future. Importantly, she wants to be ready to leave her current position and pursue her dreams without worrying about income.

Susan and her husband started a 529 college fund for their kids years ago, but they recently learned about some of its limitations such as only being able to use it for tuition and not for other college-related expenses. In addition, she and her husband have 401(k) plans that they fund at the maximum level allowed each year.

Susan and her husband want to be very well prepared for their future retirement and understand that their living expenses might escalate should they need long term care at some point that is not covered by their medical insurance.

To address all of these issues, Susan found an experienced financial planner who has skills and experience in college funding and retirement planning. Working together with this advisor, Susan's family has made a very sound financial plan to pay for college tuition and also provide for a stable retirement. The plan utilized a combination of financial products, including 401(k)/IRA, annuity, and cash value life insurance (CVLI). Their advisor will help Susan's family manage these strategies according to market trends and their specific situations.

Susan has reached a state of peace of mind about her family finances. The critical thing she learned and that you, too, can learn, is the value of getting help from a good financial planner.

Case 2: Laurie, who came from a humble background but achieved financial freedom in her early 50s

I met Laurie when she was in her early 40s. She is a single woman who is happy to share her story to help other woman learn from her experience. When we met, Laurie was a regional security manager for Starbucks. Today she still works for Starbucks – not because she has to, but because she likes the work. Let's look at her story.

Laurie came to the United States when she was 8 years old with her mom and two sisters. Without knowing the language, and without much money, they stayed in the crowded living room of her aunt's home near Chinatown in San Francisco. Laurie was a good student and knew education was the path to changing her life and her family's life. In high school, she began working as an intern for the local police department and later worked there full-time as she pursued her degree in criminal justice at San Francisco State University. She received full financial aid from the police department and, as part of the aid agreement, she continued to work there for many years after she graduated.

Laurie graduated from college in 1991, and she was making around $30k for her salary and $15k in overtime from the police department. She always saved at least 30% of her total income, putting away around $10k each year in her 20s. As her career progressed and her income increased, so did the amount she was able to save.

When she had saved enough money for a down payment, Laurie made her first smart investment, buying her first home in San Francisco. It was a three-bedroom home with about 1500 square feet. To help cover the mortgage and allow herself to keep up her saving habit, she rented two of the rooms to her coworkers. She paid $250,000 for the home in 1996. In 2020, it was valued at $1.5M.

Four or five years after purchasing her first home, Laurie had saved another $50,000 and then she made her next smart investment. In 2001, she purchased a second house in Berkeley, CA, for $100,000 – it was a true fixer upper. She invested an additional $30k in renovations and repairs and then rented that home out. Today it is valued at more than $600k.

Laurie had been watching the housing market closely which had dropped almost 40% due to the depression in the United States. In 2008, she saw the market drop and believed it would be a good time to purchase another house, although many of her friends and colleagues cautioned her that there could be further market meltdowns which would make it hard to sell. Listening to her own intuition, Laurie purchased a third house in Fremont, CA, for $200k. Once again, she made a smart move; in 2020, that house was valued at $700k.

In 2007, Laurie left the police department and joined Starbucks as a regional manager, just when the business was booming. As part of her compensation, she was offered company stock options, via a restricted stock option plan. The return on these stock options has been significant; currently the stocks she owns are worth almost $1M.

Laurie's police department work offered a pension plan and Starbucks offers a 401(k) to which she contributes 10% of her income. Over time, these plans have accumulated more than $500k for her.

After purchasing her third home, Laurie decided to focus on diversifying her investments. She met with a senior financial planner and learned how to use cash value life insurance to save money and avoid taxes.

Today, Laurie is in her 50s and this is her financial picture:

- She owns three houses in the San Francisco Bay Area with the net worth over two million dollars
- She has more than $1M invested in the stock market
- She has $500k in savings in cash value life insurance, which also provides insurance in case of critical or chronic disease or illness
- She has $500k in her 401(k) and other pension plans
- She has tens of thousands in cash saved in easily accessible bank accounts.
- Her total net worth is around $4M

Laurie's monthly expenses are about $6000 for her current lifestyle; $4000 of that is covered by her income from her rental properties after paying the mortgages. With interest revenue from her $1M in stocks, Laurie has reached financial freedom with enough passive income to cover her needs.

Here's what we can learn from Laurie, who went from humble beginnings to financial freedom and a net worth of $4M:

- Get your education and be willing to work hard. Laurie found a way to get an excellent education paid for by her employer.
- Establish a saving habit today. Laurie has always saved 30% of her income.
- Start investing early. Laurie began investing when she was in her 20s.
- Seek professional guidance to learn new things. Laurie had the confidence to try new things and learn what she didn't know so she could make her money work for her in real estate, stocks, and cash value life insurance.

Case 3: Prisha, a professional woman with a family in an expensive area

Prisha and her husband are in their early 40s and they both came to the United States from India about 15 years ago. Prisha and her husband work in high tech companies in the Silicon Valley; Prisha as a product manager, and her husband as a software engineer.

Prisha and her husband have two kids in elementary school and Prisha's parents live with them and are financially dependent upon them. Their combined annual income is about $320k. Although their income is high, their expenses are also high.

Their monthly take home is about $20k (after social security, Medicare, disability insurance, health insurance and federal and state taxes, 401(k),etc.) and their monthly expenses average $15k, leaving $5000 a month for savings.

They used to max-fund their 401(k) (which was $18,500 in 2019), to take advantage of tax deferred benefits, but after learning about other tax advantaged retirement options (such as Allianz Advantage Pro or Pacific Life Discovery products), they are now using both methods to supplement their future retirement.

Today they have a net worth of around $2.4M as outlined below:

Primary house:	$1M in equity
(the market value is $1.5M, the remaining mortgage is $500k)	
401(k):	$700k
Cash Value Life Insurance (CVLI):	$300k
Mutual fund:	$300k
College fund:	$200k
Other:	$100k

As they look toward retirement, Prisha and her husband are working with a professional financial planner who not only knows traditional mutual fund investing but also understands how to use different strategies to meet their financial goals, save on taxes, and plan for large expenses.

In addition to their retirement planning, they are also working with a college funding advisor to plan for their children's college expenses, which they anticipate being $60k per year for four years for each of their two children, a total of half a million dollars.

This is a fairly typical family in the Silicon Valley area. They are making a good income but have high expenses as well. They may not reach financial freedom for a long time, but they both have a good education and reasonable knowledge of personal finance. They also understand the importance of leveraging financial professionals to help them understand and take advantage of the latest financial products.

Below is the calculation of their retirement (or financial freedom) age:

- Current age: Prisha and her husband are both 42
- Current family income: $320,000
- Total annual savings: $80,000
- Currently accumulated assets: $2.2M (their current net asset is $2.4M, but $200k has been put aside for their college planning)

- Current lifestyle cost: $204k (current income minus taxes and annual savings)

Assume their assets grow at an annual rate of 6% until retirement and then drop to 5% during retirement due to more conservative investing to minimize market risks. Considering an average inflation rate of 3% on income and expenses, and assuming future income from Social Security (estimated at $3000 per month for each of them), Prisha and her husband can retire (or reach financial freedom) at age 57.

This knowledge gave Prisha a sense of relief and peace, knowing they could easily retire and cover their financial needs before they turn 60. She is committed to continuing to work with her financial advisors to perform the adjustments needed to reach her family's goals.

From Prisha's case study we can learn a few key things:

- Planning is very important - including financial planning, college planning, retirement planning and lifestyle planning. Planning is what gives Prisha peace of mind for her family.
- It is wise to leverage the wisdom and experience of financial professionals to help with this planning to manage money growth, market risk and future financial needs.

Takeaways from these real cases

In this chapter, we shared real life stories about three women and their families. Each woman is doing well financially. Two reached financial freedom at a relatively early age. What do they have in common? We can learn from their wise decisions:

1. Work hard to make a good income when you are young
2. Save, save, save – start saving as soon as you begin earning income
3. Invest wisely, learn continuously, and get help from qualified financial professionals

7

Financial Professionals

There are many types of financial professionals and they perform specific functions. Some professionals have multiple functional areas based on their credentials and experience. You may need to work with more than one financial professional to accomplish all of your goals. These professionals include:

1. Certified Public Accountant (CPA)
2. Registered Investment Advisor (RIA)
3. Certified Financial Advisor (CFP)
4. College Funding Advisor
5. Estate Planning Attorney
6. Retirement Planning Advisor
7. Mortgage Broker and Agent
8. Insurance Agent

Below we discuss different personal financial functions you will encounter in your life and the professionals that can help you.

1. Personal Tax Preparation

It is said that the only two certainties in life are death and taxes. And it's true - we are required to submit our tax returns each year. Many people go to CPAs, IRS Enrolled Agents (EAs), or qualified tax preparers to get their tax forms done. Some people do it themselves at home with the help of tax preparation software such as TurboTax.

Unless your finances are very straightforward, or you are a tax expert yourself, we would recommend you work with qualified tax professionals as they may provide valuable advice on current requirements and ways to reduce the tax you owe. This recommendation is especially important if you have multiple investment accounts, rental home investments, and/or businesses.

The general cost of filing personal tax forms ranges from $500 to $3000 depending on the complexity of the work. The guidance these professionals can provide, as well as the taxes you may save from their advice and knowledge, may very well justify the costs.

2. Tax Planning

Most people do not realize the importance of tax planning. Tax planning is the analysis of your personal financial situation from a tax perspective, with the purpose of ensuring maximum tax efficiency for the long term. Considerations of tax planning include timing of income and purchases and planning for expenditures, college funding and retirement planning.

Most accountants, CPAs or tax preparers help you in filing your taxes for the current year, but they may not be qualified to help you in tax planning for the next 10, 20 or more years. This is best done with the help of a Certified Financial Planner who has long-term tax planning knowledge and experience.

3. Brokerage Account Management

People generally seek help from financial professionals to manage their brokerage accounts, with the goal to accumulate wealth and minimize risks.

This type of work is done by financial advisors who have securities licenses. These financial advisors may work with corporate financial services companies, such as banks, Merrill Lynch, Morgan Stanley, Edward Jones, Charles Schwab, etc., or they may be independent financial advisers who use third party neutral financial platforms which often offer more objectivity and transparency to clients.

4. College Funding Planning

College funding planning is an emergent need, as costs for a college education continue to increase.

For big name private universities, such as Stanford, the cost of attendance has gone to about $90k per year. At lesser-known universities, it is not uncommon for costs to run more than $50k per year. Even public universities have seen rapidly increasing costs. If you have multiple children who are planning for a post-secondary education, this can become your largest expense and investment and can easily run up to $200k for each child.

There are a small number of advisors in the financial industry who are specially trained and certified in college funding planning. These professionals provide knowledge and guidance to help families plan for college funding, including:

- Calculating Expected Family Contribution (EFC), which is a measure of your family's financial strength and is calculated according to a formula established by law
- Lowering EFC legally to maximize your chance of getting college financial aid
- Making a college funding plan so you can pay college costs in the most efficient way
- Improving your overall financial position in terms of cash flow, college funding, taxes, and retirement

5. Retirement Planning

The time to plan for your retirement is years – even decades – before you reach retirement age. I recommend that people review their options and make a solid financial plan for retirement before they reach the age of 50. Retirement planning is best undertaken with financial advisors who have specific knowledge and experience with retirement planning, such as those with the Certified Financial Planner designation, as it requires more specific skills beyond those of basic financial planners.

Retirement planning includes knowledge of financial planning, estate planning, tax planning, long-term care insurance, life insurance and more. Certified Financial Planners help clients plan for their lifetime income needs and increasing costs as clients age.

6. Estate Planning

Estate planning is the process of anticipating and arranging for the management and disposal of an individual's estate during the person's life and after death, while minimizing taxes and costs related to gifts, estates, generation skipping transfers, and income. This process includes planning for incapacity as well as eliminating uncertainties over the administration of probate and maximizing the value of the estate by reducing taxes and other expenses. Typically, financial planners and estate lawyers who specialize in this area are utilized by the client to meet their specific goals, whether simple or more complex.

7. Home Mortgage and Refinance

When people buy a home, they normally put a down payment on the home and borrow the rest of the funds through a home mortgage, often through their bank. Later, they may choose to refinance to take advantage of a drop in interest rates or to take money out of the valuation to meet specific financial needs. When refinancing, most people shop around for the best rates offered by mortgage brokers or agents.

8. Insurance

Just as there are many types of insurance (home, auto, health, life, long-term care), there are many types of insurance agents you may need to work with to meet your various insurance needs.

9. Surrounding Yourself with Financial Professionals

Like any other industry, financial professionals are differentiated by their skills, experience, personal values, and work styles. Choosing the best professionals for your needs is of utmost importance for your financial health and peace of mind.

I suggest seeking referrals from trusted friends and family members for financial professionals who can provide the services you need. You can interview a few professionals in the field and make your selection using your common sense after checking their references and certifications. You can also try different professionals to determine which is the best fit for you and your family.

Most individuals and families begin seeking the help of financial professionals in their 20s and 30s as they seek out insurance coverage. And their need for professional financial guidance only grows as their income and family grows. Working with highly qualified professionals can save you time and money in the long run, including providing peace of mind that you are managing your assets and obligations well.

Most of these professionals are not expensive and some are even free to you. Many work on a commission basis which means they don't charge you for their recommendations, but the company they represent pays them a fee when you choose their products or services.

The time to start looking for financial professionals to help manage your assets and needs is when you begin earning income. If you have not yet established relationships with the professional you will need, you can get access to many qualified professionals that I have worked with for years at www.DrSherryHu.com.

Once you begin working with your professional advisors, you will be more attuned to the market and the latest financial tools available so you can catch more opportunities and minimize risks in managing your money.

8

Take Action, Make a Plan, and Reach Peace of Mind in Your Finances

Are you ready to get on your way toward peace of mind in your personal finances?

Let's get started!

Sign up at the website www.DrSherryHu.com with the code PEACEOFMIND, and you will get free access to online resources (a value of $999.00) that will help you get on the right path to reach peace of mind in your personal finances.

You will find guidance from financial professionals to help you:

1) Evaluate your current situation
2) Make a plan to improve your current situation
3) Execute the plan
4) Check your performance and progress
5) Continuously improve yourself financially

In addition, you can always ask questions to me and my team of financial professionals.

I look forward to connecting with you!

Acknowledgments

I would like to thank my family, Tom, Elizabeth, Hubert, Mingyong, Xiangfu, Rong, Chuhan, Yun and many others, for their unconditional love, deep trust, and forever support to me, no matter what I choose to take on in my life.

I would like to thank Bob Harberson, a senior financial advisor and church ministry leader, who helped to expand my knowledge in college funding planning and retirement planning.

I am also grateful to Rashim Mogha, a published author and keynote speaker, a tech woman leader in the Silicon Valley, and an inspirational friend.

I would like to thank Gwen Chew, whose courage to deal with life difficulties has deeply touched and encouraged me.

I give my gratitude to all my clients, who have deep trust in me and have allowed me to guide them in their family financial planning.

Last but not least, I want to give my thanks to Michelle Bergquist, Dianne Callahan, Bethany Kelly, and the team at Women Lead Publishing. Without them, I would not have gotten this book finished, polished and published.

Resources/For More Information

Now you have almost finished this book and you have a better understanding of the fundamentals of personal finance.

It is time to start your own exciting journey toward peace of mind in your personal finances!

If you have not registered your book online yet, please visit www.DrSherryHu.com now to claim your BONUS financial tools and resources with the code PEACEOFMIND.

Below are additional resources you may find helpful:

For College Planning:
www.BeyondAcademyCA.org

For Retirement Planning:
www.POMFinance.com

The Retirement Miracle, by Patrick Kelly
www.patrickkellybook.com

About the Author

Dr. Sherry Hu was born in the 1970s in China and raised by two well-educated parents, which was very rare during that time.

Sherry's father grew up on a farm in Hunan province and went to college as the first college student in his town in 1960. He had to overcome many challenges to attend college as his family was very poor and often hungry. He lost his mom when he was just three years old and did not enter school until he was ten.

He understood that the only way to change his life and his family's life was through education He studied extremely hard at school and earned an exceptional opportunity to attend college.

Sherry's mother experienced drought, starving, wars, and dramatic family changes in her childhood. Her father, Sherry's grandpa, was a respected high school teacher in a mid-sized town in Hubei, China, and Sherry's grandma was a typical woman of the time in

China, hardworking, kind, brave, and tenacious. She was determined to see that Sherry's mother received an education no matter how difficult it was.

When Sherry was young, her family's budget was very tight, like most families during that period of time in China. However, Sherry always felt fortunate because they had enough food and warm clothing during those years.

She learned a critically important financial habit from her parents early in her life. Her parents always planned how much to spend based on how much they earned and never went above. They always saved more than 20% of their salaries, no matter how much they made or how difficult life was.

Current data show that about 70% of Americans have less than $1000 savings in their bank accounts, which could be less than the cost of a car repair. The interesting contrast is about 50% of people in China have savings - this is just one of many good habits Chinese families carry on from their traditions.

Sherry came to the United States in her mid-20s and went to University of Nebraska-Lincoln where she earned her PhD degree. In 2004, she started as an assistant professor at the University of Nevada, Las Vegas. She and her husband had two children and began planning for their family's financial needs, They bought a new home, a new van, and started retirement accounts at work. They saved 15-30% of their income and began investing in stocks. By her mid-20s, Sherry and her family were thriving. She also kept up the habit of learning her parents impressed upon her.

Dr. Sherry Hu has talked to more than 50 financial professionals, taken at least 1000 hours of training, studied 100+ books and completed thousands of case studies, and she has finally figured out the best method for personal finances.

Using this method, she has reached financial freedom and gained peace of mind along with it. This is why she wrote this book. She wants to share this method with you.

After reading this book and applying its concepts to your life, Dr. Sherry Hu believes you can reach peace of mind in your personal finances too!

About Women Lead Publishing

Women Lead Publishing is a hybrid publishing company dedicated to serving female authors. Our passion is to give voice, credibility, and influence to authors with a mission and purpose of expanding their thought leadership and impact through published works.

Women Taking Charge Series

The Women Taking Charge series consists of short-read books designed to elevate credibility, influence, and impact for subject matter experts. The series is focused on leadership, business, the workplace, life, and money.

52 Tips Series

The 52 Tips series comprises concise, powerful tips books designed to elevate credibility, influence, and impact for subject matter experts on a variety of subjects or themes.

Made in the USA
Monee, IL
04 November 2026

67381299R00066